GW00372168

# Strands of Silk

## Shed Poets

BP

First published in Ireland in 2010

Text © the authors

Published by Boland Press
Co. Wexford
Ireland

A CIP catalogue record for this book
is available from the British Library

ISBN 978 1 907855 00 9


http://shedpoetssociety.blogspot.com



The Shed Poets gratefully acknowledge
financial assistance from
Dun Laoghaire-Rathdown County Council




Cover photograph by Peadar O'Donoghue
Cover design by Carol Boland


Printed by Conway Media Limited

**The Shed Poets Society**
meets each week
in a terraced garden
overlooking Killiney Bay.

*Strands of Silk*
is the group's fourth
collection of poems.

# Foreword

## Poetry should never be boring

Poetry should never be boring. If it is, then it isn't poetry. Poets should be fearless and should write about real things. This collection, the fourth such publication from a group of writers who have been meeting each week for seven years now, fulfils all of these provisos and more. The voices of the six writers remain as splendidly and unforcedly their own, as individual as are the six women themselves.

What they do have in common is the knowledge of how to put a poem together, of how to inhabit the recording of experience until it is unignorable, human and true, with wit and self-aware under-standing. As in Bernie Kenny's Birthday, *You're telling me/what I should know, yet I believe/I am still too young to be old/... Until I am old – and that will be/decided when I get there - /I'll wear long vintage dresses/in alarming colours.* Or the epiphany of Marguerite Colgan's lacemakers, the seabirds who stitch the... rock of the Little Skellig, *Choirs of gannets rasp and bark/congregate in family pews/some hover overhead,/black tips on angel wings.*

There is a motif of haunted and haunting numi-nous lyricism throughout, particularly when fac-ing the terrible demands which life inevitably makes. From the anguish of Maureen Perkins' Mirror mirror on the wall, *My baby's face is not snow-white/her hair is more the raven's wing/but I smell roses in her skin/...I cry. How white the winter is./We hold our snow-white, say good-bye/her cradle now a casket* through to Rosy Wilson's Waterborne, juxtaposing birth and death, *pulled beyond/limits, crashed onto rocks/and would have gone under./They wrapped me in silver,/I wear a broken ring finger/rough sea reminder.*

A motif slightly retuned but no less present in Carol Boland's adroitly referential song, Still dancing, *Are you still dancing in the dark/in two bare feet/paying no heed/without watch or breath/in the stillness of the undergrowth* and in Judy Russell's intricately realized and mysterious gloss on Botticelli's Birth of Venus: On the brink, *Surely not long from now/I will be lithe again and fleet of foot,/run leaping down the rugged mountain side/melt in the sweetness of fulfilled desire,/put to sea in a shell and let the wind take me.*

A collection which reveals over and over the dangerous joy of dealing unashamedly and fearlessly, for better or worse, with the myriad possibilities of the real.

Macdara Woods
June 2010

# CONTENTS

## Judy Russell

## Rosy Wilson

## Marguerite Colgan

## Bernie Kenny

## Carol Boland

## Maureen Perkins

## Notes

**Judy Russell** is a published
poet and playwright. She
lives in the valley of
Glencree, Co. Wicklow.

## As black clouds gather

rain spits tinny drops
on the empty watering can,
butterflies dart frantic for cover.

The birds have gone quiet,
thunder prowls along the ridge,
as black clouds gather

a rocking girl stops up her ears,
the post man pedals past
mumbling
half forgotten prayers
under his breath
as black clouds gather.

**Judy Russell**

## New Year's Eve

on a full moon, a blue moon,
the valley lies steeped in snow light
no breath of wind stirs trees
the black river flows soundless
between downy banks
below the cabin, past the island
where the sheep jumped in
and drowned. A shadow fox
with black-tipped tail pads by.

Granite mountains ring.

The seemly silence splits,
a pheasant's screech, soon spent,
death cry to the singing stars.

**Judy Russell**

## Drowning in sound

Great whales power along the coast
northward from Baja,
singing lullabies to newborn calves
curved cadences
muted and pitched to echo through oceans
thousands of miles.

Clacking dolphins, snapping shrimp,
extemporize with slapping waves,
play staccato as the wind
caresses sea skin
tosses spray manes and boisterous birds
glistened in spume.

Shipping and drilling,
sonar and seismic, war-games and profits
rip through fluid fabric,
mutilate cries, leave giants stranded
on gritty shores.

**Judy Russell**

## Hear this, my children

from an old woman who remembers
fish from a fishmonger
wrapped in yesterdays news,
filmy-eyed cods heads
for Bella and Bagpuss.

The grocer scooped rice, tea,
sugar from barrels
to be weighed on the counter,
poured into blue paper bags
with the sound of surf
dragging pebbles down a beach.

Glass milk bottles clattered
onto the doorstep
in time for porridge,
cream rich gold tops
plundered by birds.

Now food comes cased in plastic
vacuum packed, sits in plastic trays.
Plastic migrates uncontrolled

**Judy Russell**

blows in the wind,
snags on bushes, trees,
straggles roadsides
clogs rivers and streams
slides torn away down to the sea

by slipstreams and eddies
sucking and drifting
to the great oceans' vortex,
the world's plastic convenes
where five million tons

five million tons

of polymer chowder twice bigger than Texas
cheats sea birds and fish
tourniquets turtles

returns to us dioxin rich delicacies,
mercury soup.

**Judy Russell**

## Hiatus

My mind moves slowly dragged by dreams,
inhaling lilac, morning sun.
A wasp rasps its tongue stripping pine,
nesting time. That bossy bullfinch scolds
my sloth, no seeds nor porridge oats
pile his picnic table, all the while
the rippling river, scented breeze,
seduce attention and indulge delay.

Let me ignore the screaming from the oubliette,
be safely wrapped in peace some moments yet.

**Judy Russell**

## Moonlight

The blue T.V. light flickers in the window
as I stand outside, breathing in roses.

My father travelled to work by train,
worked long hours, a half-day Saturday,
but on moonlit nights we'd walk
out of the town, up over the common,
a windmill's bare arms praising the sailing stars,
and climb the hill to the woods
where beech trees stood ankle-deep
in crisp leaves. Night creatures paused
as we passed through the disembodied dusk
pale moon lighting our way.

Tonight's crescent dangles Venus,
blazing in a blood-streaked sky.

**Judy Russell**

## On the brink

I stalk the seashore like a hungry beast
waiting to be young again,
up to my ankles in the chill sea foam
toes in the satin sand
while others ride the surf and crest the wave.

Surely not long from now
I will be lithe again and fleet of foot,
run leaping down the rugged mountain side
melt in the sweetness of fulfilled desire,
put to sea in a shell and let the wind take me.

**Rosy Wilson** is a published
poet and active member of
poetry groups in Dublin and
London. Her first collection,
*Under the Sugarloaf,* was
published in 2006.

## Silk thread of friendship

For Judy

This morning after last night's rain
broken sunshine casts reflections
on a grey silk road stretching under
silver birch and elderberry trees
from my back door to yours.

Your butter-coloured smock
chosen in a multi-culture market
is Chinese silk embroidered with
green flowers, leaves.  You wear it
in harmony with long blonde hair.

**Rosy Wilson**

## Water borne

September sunlight silvers
aquamarine, oystercatchers
run on sparkling shingle
I swim in calm water.

Three Sundays earlier
Rosalina was born from
your breaking waters
cried her first breath of air.

It's hard to remember that
three years before I swam
in despair, pulled beyond
limits, crashed onto rocks

and would have gone under.
They wrapped me in silver,
I wear a broken ring finger
rough sea reminder.

**Rosy Wilson**

## Haiku December 2008

1.Winter sunrise

salmon, mother of pearl
clouds rib sky, pattern sea
cover my leaving.

2. After swim

spine stretches vertebrae
on slats of cedar wood sauna
mind floats on hot air.

3. Stormy weather

charcoals stone wall sky
brown waves break, few surfers
dare ride their crests.

4. On the edge

mind-numbing winds
blow me towards sea boulders
tumbling cliffs of breakers.

5. Leaving the hospital

I drive home into
a giant copper moon which
tips the horizon.

## Seeking Solace

Boots crunch snow
up Carraigoona
reach the cairn

we face east watch
marigold sunrise
over blue lead sea

on our west are
Wicklow Hills folding
towards the Sally Gap

to the south more
mountains, Lugnaquilla
longest, hardest climb

northwards Howth
stretches one arm
holding Dublin Bay.

We need to greet this day
occasion of ancient prayer
ask pardon of our planet

for failure to take measures
which may save, nourish
every living part of earth.

**Rosy Wilson**

We search for exorcism
sins of the Fathers who
harm little children

millstones round their
collared necks
ours are bent.

Turning we look inwards
sadness of the year,
your son's illness

my husband's passing,
takes its toll, loneliness as
Christmas looms on the horizon.

    Sun climbs higher
    dazzles snow, ice
    this winter solstice.

**Rosy Wilson**

## I dream tonight

you are beside
me in the bed

turn over quietly
not to disturb your sleep

stretch a gentle arm
around your shoulder

hug empty air where
your firm flesh should be

as though a hare
has loped over the edge

a heron's flown from
its familiar tree.

**Rosy Wilson**

## A bunch of poets at Caheraderry

a backdrop of roses
ivory, blush, deep pink,
perfumes and lights the garden
where women write:

under a blue sunhat
Maureen consults
her leaflets, pens her poem
silent concentration;

Carol's hat is broad-rimmed
circled with a red ribbon
of imagination, she scribbles
words that fly

and Judy's are like swallows
arriving from Africa to
the Burren, her pirate scarf
is blue with white spots;

Marguerite's head is covered
with a wavy black hat
making lacy patterns on her paper
where her pen moves in waves;

indoors Bernie sits alone
at a round table out-writing us all.
I am watching them
blessed by their presence.

## Woodsman

For Davey


Wood is good
theme song
of your sculpture
in an exhibition.

On Greystones beach
you arrange sea shells
a CND symbol circled
with drift wood.

Beech whips dug
into mulched earth
grow up strong
a copper hedge.

Logs sawn, split,
stored under eaves
warm your hearth
keep our fire alive.

In a wicker cradle
near your sanded bed
the notion of wood
murmurs early words.

**Marguerite Colgan** is a member of Bealtaine Writers. She has read at poetry events in Dublin and Wicklow.

## Tumbleweed in the Wides

They bounce along the land in light air,
rolling past me, silent as angels,
shy as will o'the wisps.

Goosegrass blades with carmine stripe,
in sunshine, sucked life from deep below.

Yellow, sere, earth let them go,
laid them down, earth to earth.

Wind rises the straw ribbons,
blows them, shakes off the dust,
fashions lace balloons,

sets them free
to dance cartwheels across dry land,
no need for rain or sun,

        tumbling over

           tumbling over.

**Marguerite Colgan**

## Wars' Witness

To execute my shot
no need to pull the trigger,
destroy life.
I take aim, snap, catch,
still the action,
blot out the scream of death,
the stench.
Released on paper
this will outlive me,
outlive this war.

Today a soldier stands,
gun resting by his thigh,
legs apart, at ease,
rooted by strong boots
a colossus towering over innocence.
I crouch to capture the crouching family
barefoot amid shards of pottery and grit,

an older woman guarding children,
all watch through big eyes, open mouths,
images posed by fear and wonder,
I see lines, curves, shadows.
And it's still life.

**Marguerite Colgan**

## Bald eagle

An old cottontree traces trunk and limbs,
skeletal, across bare blue winter sky,
a bald eagle, blacksheen cloak, white hood
perches on the highest twig.

The sacred bird looks over his America,
land older than the united states.
Once it was prairie home to the red-man,
crossed by pioneers on Waggon Road
inching West.
The Big Dry Creek flows still a slow stream.

Tumbleweed hurtles by as always
prairie dogs whoop their sundance, now
coyotes keep shy distance as tarmac
and rubber tyres crisscross this plain,
the strip mall, McDonald's,
the village new-planted.

Does he notice us purring by in the red mustang.

**Marguerite Colgan**


## Her Westport


The town fostered her, the little girl,
plucked from her island home, her family,
for schooling with older cousins
and an ageing aunt.

I see the house, three storeys high,
painted green,
over the empty shop-front, the name
picked out in yellow,
though Sean Malone is bones for decades,

only sun lights these windows now. The street
rises steep with a curl of houses,
hair salon, flower shop, ghostly laughs and
running feet of the High Street girls.

By the Mall the Carrowbeg still sparkles gold
to the Quay and the Atlantic. A convent gate,
padlocked, tells no tales from school.

Holidays saw her back home in Achill,
ties of blood, sea and Sliabhmór,
a visitor here too, calling on cousins, neighbours
while siblings leave for Cleveland one by one.

**Marguerite Colgan**

I walk the litany:
Mill Street, Bridge Street,
Altamount and James
from the wild fuchsia days of her youth.

The train pulls away, I leave behind
my mother's town,
the what-ifs.

**Marguerite Colgan**

## Did they die, these island folk

who piled stone on stone to shelter
animal and man, tilled thin soil
at the weather's whim,

'times they swept the ash, closed the door,
left to build on higher ground or
across the waves planted again,

these Achill men, thin and brown as twig,
strong women holding all together,
girl shoulders held old head.

Did they die, turn to bone
in Kildomhnait, Sliabhmór, Cleveland,

or do their spirits blow
with the north-westerly, howl down
old chimney on cloud-flying night,
rise with brown trout on Keel lake,
lark-sing in high blue, no wing,
moondance silver on the ocean.

Waves hurry foam messages,
spill them in long hand over sand,
spray salt again, again across soft green bog.

22

**Marguerite Colgan**

## The Little Skellig

A sandstone cathedral looms.
Storm carves pew-ledge, minaret, spire,
drenches them, blows them dry.
Ridged buttress arches into the deep.

Choirs of gannets rasp and bark
congregate in family pews
some hover overhead,
black tips on angel wings.

High sunshine beckons the lacemakers.
They take their places,
stitch the island rock, row on row
a tracery of white knots, grey picot,
smudge guano for a backing veil.

With forward eyes, beaks needle sharp,
the stitchers crosshatch, loop
figures of eight, swoop to settle a knot.
Another and another rises.

**Marguerite Colgan**

## The Field

after a painting by Basil Bradshaw.

He paints his moments at the field
tears the brown earth open
strands gold through barley straw

stretches a wide acre, hints
a hollow where rain might hold,
no crows, no man in sight.

Was this oak forest when the ice slipped north,
did hunters settle, clear and plant seed,
watch at Samhain, Imbolg, Lunasa.

Desperate fingers scrabbled at clay and
finding only decay added their bones.

This man killed for his field,
that pair never talked with fifty years,

another farmer owns it now, says it's his,
works it with the seasons
raw sienna, burnt sienna, umber yellow.

**Bernie Kenny** holds an M.A. in
Creative Writing (Poetry).
Her published books include
*Poulnabrone* ('02), *Progeny* ('04),
*Isle of Thorns* ('06),
*A Walk in Dalkey* ('08) and
translations from Irish in
*Gone to Earth* ('05).

## When I peel onions

I cry for the child I was,
playing with chanies
finding late strawberries
and getting in the way
while father saved his onion crop
spread it out to dry.

All winter long
plucked from Gallic traces,
onions flavoured soup, stews
and every savoury thing.

On Lenten Fridays they
made dinner sautéed in butter
with parsley sauce, potatoes,
pepper, salt, great appetites.

For Easter Day boiled onion skins
dyed our hard-boiled eggs
Rhode Island red and we were eight
around the breakfast table
when the sun danced.

**Bernie Kenny**

## All Souls

From every corner comes the hum
of 'how've you been' and 'did you hear',
spangles of laughter, champagne toasts,
hints of scandal, tall stories.

Against night spells
we close the doors, until
a charm of mini-witches,
devils, spidermen comes
trick or treating in a whoosh
of shrivelled leaves.

Fireworks cackle and hiss
and like a dance macabre
a wild wind waltzes
with stripped twigs
and the moon is full.

No ghost sits at our feast
but thoughts of a loved one gone
float on buoyant spirits
and we say – it seems
like yesterday she was
the life and soul of our party.

**Bernie Kenny**

## November

In this morning's post
I receive unbidden

the penny catechism of my youth,
same blue-green cover,
pages tissue-thin, numbered
one to sixty-three,
all asking, answering
questions on the cosmic why
of our existence

and I am a child again,
uncomprehending,
learning every page by heart,
sing-song replies verbatim,
big words, big lists, big sins
– seven deadly –
on the tip of my tongue.

Behind Killiney Hill the sun
sets earlier each day
and I am mindful of you,
at peace when the end drew near,
you simply said –
we must believe.

**Bernie Kenny**

## Birthday

With gratitude I accept your seat
on the crowded bus. You're telling me
what I should know, yet I believe
I am still too young to be old.

Older yes. Glimpsed from behind
might I be mistaken for, say, sixty-nine
or seventy, or at the most, not a day
over seventy-five.

That withered woman
in the mirror I do not recognise,
am I not too hopeful, too busy,
too insufficiently wise.

You advise I do more resting.
With help from some spare parts
I consider myself fit, but promise
to avoid as best I can

being required to wear
life jackets, thermal underwear, skis,
or go on African safaris to stare
at fierce photogenic beasts.

**Bernie Kenny**

Until I am old – and that will be
decided when I get there –
I'll wear long vintage dresses
in alarming colours,

trust my shopping trolley
with essentials and now and then
recall the auburn girl
who danced with life.

turned her back and waltzed away.
Imagine her surprise
if she could see me now
at eighty-five.

**Bernie Kenny**

## If you've been to Lisdoonvarna

to take the waters and gagged
on a glass of sulphur water,
then spare a thought for Rotorua,

where that smell pervades
a geothermal moonscape
of geysers, fumaroles, hissing vents,

of Maori myth and mystery,
the past a constant presence
in a yellow stench.

Watch your step as you skirt
the Devil's Cauldron, a brown pool
belching boiling mud,

Champagne Lake where acid-green,
alizarin, coolblue, crystalise
in clouds of steam.

**Bernie Kenny**

In haunted dark, spy on sightless
Kiwi, arrow-beaked, hen-sized,
larger than you thought.

Dine if you dare on Hangi kai,
meat earth-oven-cooked by heated rocks,
as the Fianna did in their Fulacht Fia.

**Bernie Kenny**

## On holiday in the City of Sails

I'm spoiled for choice, say no
to surfing, snorkelling, scuba diving,
will not venture out
on speedboat, kayak, dinghy,
wear wet-suit or life-jacket.
Here without a plan,
I have no bus to catch,

all day to find roads new to me,
they welcome me with sun.
I listen to their Maori names,
Wapiti, Aratonga, Remuera,
smell butter-yellow roses
in a Papakura garden.

On Waihi beach, shells gleam,
sea like glass, weather perfect
and I am breathing.  Yes,
my word-picture may not be tactile
or gushing like a juicy peach,
but open the door,
expect a poem on the breeze.

**Bernie Kenny**

## Ode to Light

Until I had my cataract removed

bluebells were blue.  Now in each flower
my new-seeing eye finds sapphire

edged with sky, and stamens
are bell-pulls dipped in gold,

a granite wall shows glints of mica,
grains of feldspar and quartz

and, puddling a reflection, cherry blossom
paints a watercolour on the path.

I think of Monet losing his sight,
waiting too late,

an artist entranced by the garden he made,
mutations of light

on plant, pond, sky.  I feel his rage
kicking his boot

through canvases of water lilies,
in despair.

His vision remains, mine to view.

**Carol Boland** is a
performance poet and
editor of *The Space Inside
Arts Journal.* Her novel
*Hostage* was published
in 2002.

## Sorcery in Caheraderry

The home grows from a ring fort
through the clay of Caheraderry
as we fish lines of syllables
from grey Liscannor stone.

Across a marshy field, flag irises
shine through this greener grass
oversee the lift and return
of two coffin stools

legs turned vermicular and
splayed to take the load -
appanages of dignity that lightly
held a master's weight a month ago.

And like the sorcerer's apprentice
we witness the breaking of a spell
as coffin stools turn back
into occasional tables.

**Carol Boland**

## Still dancing

Are you still dancing in the dark
in stocking feet
humming Cohen in a halleluiah key
that never opened doors
nor cell of your confinement.


Are you still dancing in the dark
or on a hospital trolley
holes in your socks
skin unevenly stitched
having forced your will
on an unwary Citroen.


Are you still dancing in the dark
in two bare feet
paying no heed
without watch or breath
in the stillness of the undergrowth.

**Carol Boland**

## Memories in a mattress

I wrestle the writhing beast
through the door
heave and pull
at dip and lip
until sullen and withdrawn
winded on its back
it submits in the back garden.

I stand at the foot
of this double-sided slice of my life.
So, it has come to this -
twenty years of seeping
blood, milk and tears.

I press the unseen knife to its belly
where each blemish is an act of love,
or a tainted stain
like a birthmark on a pelt
a storyboard
a hide for acts of treason.
Murder on my mind,
I stab the sagging skin
rip open its lumpy recess
spill its guts
discolour the soil
black and white.

**Carol Boland**

And up to my elbow in pleasure
I feel it squeal under my hand
as I reach for its backbone
to dislodge curls of coiled springs

condemn our shared memories
to the grave.

**Carol Boland**

## The blue mountain

A spit of snow lies on Croghan's face
jilted after the cold snap
that left parishes standing
like Miss Havisham in her mottled gown.
It needs snow to move snow, they say
so in expectation I watch for a battleship sky
to snag itself on the blue peak
scarred by chainsaw
damaged forests, promises
while below me
the river Bann cuts
through reeds and
green willow as
I trace the line of its curve,
rush of shallows
silence of its deep
imagine how it feels to walk
over mud-raked copper fields
and slip into the naked water
step by step.

Back on the road again
I stand at an altered hedgerow
swollen with marigold gloves
broken bottles, crushed vows
gather them up for the tip.

Carol Boland

## Attending the opera in Prague

I walk on squares of toffee
block against Czech block
shade against ground-breaking shade
taste the sticky days of '89.
Now gentiles fill the Jewish quarter
Kafka balances
on headless shoulders and
a socialist museum caresses
the velvet revolution.

A water-curtain falls
like a gossamer wave –
a buoyancy aid for nymphs
for Rusalka
who sings for love on terra firma
barters with her voice.

While three seats over
the golden tones of violins
catch in the throat of
a woman smiling
over an anxious mask.

Carol Boland

## The orphanage

The road from Kandy to Pinnawala
is plagued by choking buses, tuk-tuks and dogs.
Our driver knows where to park his four-by-four
our ark of cooled conditioned air.

Skins ooze factor fifty and insect repellent
as we navigate a lane awash with
bottled water and elephant dung
to the sweating slabs of Maha Oya river

where disconnected pachyderms bathe.
Wounded, lost, separated from the herd
they are led unrestrained for a splash
among the boulders,
a twice-daily ritual to wash behind the ears.

Sipping tea, we watch timeless baby jumbos
hold each other under water, wave trunks
with minds of their own.
Here, one scatters cameras with a mock charge.
There, a missing foot stolen by a land mine
reminds us of tigers crouching in the shallows.

**Carol Boland**

## Fanning the Flame

I twirl him in a butterfly net
as he circles my hair
on multi-coloured wings
of possibilities

until the strain of the last game
snaps me like a string of worry beads
scatters my alternatives
bouncing them high
and low
on a stone cold floor.

The only time he visits now
is on rumours of his wildness.

**Maureen Perkins** is a
founder member of
Bealtaine Writers.
She has an M.A. in Creative
Writing, from Queens
University, Belfast.

## She chose the rose

You live in oracle song
arouse the wisdom of sages
whose stories sing
in the lilt of your pen.

Through your epics
Cú Chulainn stalks
in rhyme upon rhyme
a hero alive in the Táin.

Maude Gonne at Howth station
you knelt at her feet
but her heart only listened
to a marching beat.

## Horse Mirrored

after Barry Flanagan

O spirit shall I call you deity
or but a wandering being
from the ocean of the night
transcending to what you will.

Lover of the deep you canter
waves of seething spray,
rear to a blood red moon
struck by lunar ecstasy.

Let me drape you with
a wreath of wild olive leaf
fly to Phideas in Olympus
and sing the odes of Pindar.

**Maureen Perkins**

## The Burren

Not Praeger's dried skeleton
more Yeats' hills of agate and jade
celebrate limestone in infinite space
a mythic brooding moonscape,

scailps like terraced rock gardens,
amphibious rivers above and below
through the dripping limestone dark,
hear their springs, music of Orpheus.

Poulnabrone dolmen rears its pagan
head, a place of the dead
on plateau of tinkling pavements,
blue gentian, mossy saxifrage.

Linger. See the skylark soar
find peace in flower and stone.

**Maureen Perkins**

**Mirror mirror on the wall**

1

My baby's face is not snow-white
her hair is more the raven's wing
but I smell roses in her skin.

Now a brooding hen my daughter
forgets she never wanted children –
no more worry about kith and kin.

Two eyes drawn from ultrasound
moon-morsel cradled in a bubble
you are the fairest of us all.

2

Shadows cross my daughter's face
the hardest days we've ever spent
no power on earth can wake

our child from her eternal sleep
face quiescent, stoic, deep.
I cry. How white the winter is.

We hold our snow-white, say goodbye
her cradle now a casket,
a red rose, wreaths of gorse
yellow on the Blackemore.

**Maureen Perkins**

## Out of the Realm of Shade

Blue black threatens the northern sky
the sun in a burst lights the hillside
gulls silvered in a spiral on high
suppose like these I could iridise.

**Maureen Perkins**

## Rathlin

On the sea journey between
Antrim and Argyle an island tells
stories of Bruce and the spider,
the defeat of Bonny Prince Charlie,
Richard Branson's drop-down balloon.

Moby Dick spray on the
ferry boat, swirls currents
boiling underneath, look out
on basalt cliffs, pink in the sunset,
greetings of strangers at Port an Draighlin.

Invasion and famine
created the island people,
upper end Gaelic, as wild
and untamed as the puffins,
Scots to the south in bible grasp.

Poets gather in The Manor House
sing stories of haunting
Ceannann Dubh, Fionnula
in the storm sea of Moyle,
Roger Casement, Louis MacNeice.

**William Orpen**

after Michael Hartnett's 'Death of an Irish Woman'


Greedy in that he overvalued riches
generous in the sense he shared his art
with eager students, knew that
what passed for patriotism was often
away with the fairies. Nevertheless
he loved his country, clenched his hands
around his world as he found it.

He was night that craved the light.
He was the realist that mocked the Celtic Twilight.
He was fashion in high places.
He was a caricaturist of the famous.
He was a caricaturist of himself.
He was the Pepys of the Western Front.
He was the tears of a war to end wars.
He was the tears of a war that didn't end wars.

## Notes

**Drowning in sound**
Baja – Off the west coast of Mexico

**Woodsman**
CND - Campaign for Nuclear Disarmament

**The Little Skellig**
picot - a series of small embroidered loops
forming an ornamental edging on lace
guano – excrement of seabirds

**The Field**
Samhain, Imbolg, Lunasa – Ancient Irish festivals

**When I peel onions**
chanies – pieces of broken crockery
traces – string of onions

**If you've been to Lisdoonvarna** and
**The City of Sails** are set in New Zealand
alizarin – a distinctive red colour
Fulacht Fia – Neolithic outdoor cooking pit

**Sorcery in Caheraderry**
Caheraderry is in County Clare
Appanages – an inheritance due to a younger son

**Are you still dancing**
Cohen – songwriter Leonard Cohen

**The blue mountain**
Croghan – mountain on the Wexford/Wicklow
border also known as the blue mountain

**Attending the Opera in Prague**
Rusalka – An opera by Dvorak based on the
Little Mermaid story

**The orphanage**
Elephant orphanage in Sri Lanka

**She chose the rose**
This poem refers to W.B. Yeats' love for Maude
Gonne, an Irish revolutionary.
Táin – early Irish legend

**Horse Mirrored** after Barry Flanagan
Barry Flanagan – contemporary sculptor known
for his giant hare statues placed outdoors.
Phideas – great sculptor of Ancient Greece
Pindar – ancient Greek poet

**The Burren**
Praeger – leading Irish naturalist
Poulnabrone dolmen – megalithic tomb

**Rathlin**
Ceannann Dubh  - mythical black horse
Orpheus – musician and poet of Greek myth.

## Acknowledgements

*Ode to light* by Bernie Kenny
was read on RTE radio.

*Seeking solace* by Rosy Wilson
was published in Bray Arts Journal Iss 7 Vol 15